Elias Nason

A Monogram on Our National Song

Elias Nason

A Monogram on Our National Song

ISBN/EAN: 9783337002442

Printed in Europe, USA, Canada, Australia, Japan

Cover: Foto ©Thomas Meinert / pixelio.de

More available books at **www.hansebooks.com**

A

MONOGRAM

ON

OUR NATIONAL SONG.

BY THE

Rev. ELIAS NASON, M.A.

"—— CONDISCE MODOS, AMANDA
VOCE QUOS REDDAS : MINUENTUR ATRAE
CARMINE CURAE. *Horace*, Car., lib. iv, car. xi.

"I KNEW A VERY WISE MAN THAT BELIEVED THAT IF A MAN WERE
PERMITTED TO MAKE ALL THE BALLADS, HE NEED NOT CARE WHO
SHOULD MAKE THE LAWS OF A NATION." *Andrew Fletcher.*

ALBANY:
JOEL MUNSELL.
1869.

A MONOGRAM

OUR NATIONAL SONG.

I. OF THE MINISTRY AND POWER OF MUSIC.

" Be sure there's something coldly wrong
About the heart that does not glow
To hear its own, its native song."

Music is a mysterious agent chiming grandly
into this world's magnificent drama and im-
parting something of life and splendor to its ever
shifting scenes.   The universe itself, which for
its harmony[1] the Greeks denominated κόσμος —
beauty, is but a royal harp—bird-strings, wind-
strings, star-strings, swept by the invisible fingers of the illustrious Composer himself, and
throwing up sparkles of spray from the vast
tone-ocean, rolling far beyond, to cheer the

---

[1] Plato asserts that the soul of the world is conjoined with
musical proportion ; Sir Isaac Newton held that the princi-
ples of harmony pervade the universe, adducing as a proof

heart of man and give him some bright earnest of felicities to come. The grand Master of music is ever sending forth his bold anthems from the echoing mountains over which the pealing thunder breaks; from the woodlands rocked by tempests; from the ever-heaving sea;—he softens these wild symphonies by the gentle song of the nightingale, the whispering of the reeds and the dying cadences of the ` evening breeze;—he also gives man power to mingle in the general concert, with his own sweet strains of vocal or of instrumental music, and thus by the ministry of art enhance the common song.

From the inexhaustible fountain of music he permits us to draw special strains for special ends; and these sometimes steal into the interior kingdom of the soul with power almost irresistible, unlock the cells of memory and

---

of this the analogy subsisting between color and sound. So Shakespeare says : [*Merchant of Venice*, Act V, Scene 1.]

"There's not the smallest orb which thou beholdest,
But in his motion like an angel sings,
Still choiring to the young-eyed cherubims;
Such harmony is in immortal souls;
But whilst this muddy vesture of decay
Doth grossly close it in, we cannot hear it."

perform angelic marvels for the way-worn and the weary.

Now a touch of some cunning harper summons wandering reason to its throne ; now an Italian Tarantella, quick and joyous, allays the poison of a viper's sting; now a captive's plaintive melody melts a tyrant into tears and moves him to unbind the chains of slavery; now some Ranz des Vâches [1] from Alpine horn makes the poor Swiss soldier pant and die for home ; now a battle march or pibroch from a Highland bagpipe turns the tide of war, and now a Marseillaise, uprising as the swell of ocean, from a hundred thousand sons of liberty shakes a throne and shapes the destiny of an empire.

We underrate, I apprehend, the power of patriotic song. That Marseillaise was called by Lamartine, the *firewater* of the old French revolution. It has several times been banished

---

[1] Airs played on a long trumpet called the alp-horn by the mountaineers of Switzerland. J. J. Rousseau relates that these strains were so dear to the Swiss in the French armies that the bands were forbidden to play them under penalty of death, since they caused the Helvetians to desert or die of what they called *la maladie du pays.*—*Moore's Cyc. Music, in loco.*

from the kingdom as an *institution* quite too
strong for kings manage; and in the late up-
heaving of the masses in our own beloved land,
I sometimes thought the grand old patriotic
peal of *Hail Columbia,* the heart thrilling war
song of the *Star Spangled Banner,* exercised a
mightier sway than any other single cause
whatever. The name of our illustrious leader
acted as a charmed spell; the favoring smiles
of beauty sent electric energy through the soldier's heart; the stars and stripes still fanned
the sacred flame; but the rousing notes of our
national patriotic music—whether rising from
the mighty congregation—organs and voices
joining, or from the black war-ship on the
moon-lit ocean, or from the screaming fife and
pealing drum upon the tented field, struck
deeper chords and moved to nobler daring.
Hence the leaders of the late rebellion were
compelled to ostracize our national songs in
order to keep their cause in countenance with
the people. *Yankee Doodle* must be silenced
ere the brave old flag could be cut down. So
long as its rich, rolicksome notes came rolling
out, the stars and stripes must float.

II. The Secret of the Power of Patriotic Song.

1. Were we to ask the secret of this transcendent power of patriotic song, I think it would be found consisting mainly in the principle of association of ideas — of ideas so completely correlated that the latter of necessity brings up a long and brilliant train which, in the hallowed glow of feeling music only can impart, come trooping in upon the mind with a redoubled strength and splendor.

A patriotic song is an enchanted key to memory's deepest cells; it touches secret springs, it kindles sacred flames in chambers of the soul unvisited by other agencies. It wakes to life ten thousand slumbering chords and makes them thrill and pulsate—just as if some loving angel's finger touched them — to the grand God-given sentiment of liberty.

A patriotic song, like the enchanter's magic wand, calls up the honored forms from

"Fame's eternal camping ground;"

it makes the immortal patriots live and breathe
again; reveals the long lines of gleaming bayo-
nets on the battle-field; renews the headlong
charge of the impetuous cavalry; repeats again
the wild huzza of the invincible phalanx of the
infantry; makes us hear once more the exulting scream of victory, and points our moistened
eye to the torn and bloodied flag still fluttering
in the breeze, and to the nation, rocked by the
scathing tempest, righting itself once more beneath the rainbow of enchanting peace flung
sweetly over it.

We hear a patriotic song in boyhood from
the lips of an honored sire who has filled our
greedy ear with the wild adventures of his old
campaigns; we listen to the rousing strain on
some cold winter evening by the ample hearth-
stone — the rude queen's arm with battered
stock, still hanging in its leathern loop above
the mantle piece — we hear the grand old stories and each note of music then becomes a
chain of gold linked with the deeds of heroes —
Adams, Warren, Schuyler, Washington.

We hear the song again in riper years — it
opens the flood-gates of patriotic feeling, and

gilds it with the sunniest dreams of our young, bounding life.

The nation in its glory, with its imposing cavalcade of *illustrissimi*, marches along before the eye of finest fancy, and rises heaven-crowned to its magnificent destiny!

2. Again, a patriotic song, as the old Marseillaise, is the embodiment of a nation's grandest thought. . It ever springs, Minerva-like, out of some dreadful exigence. It is a child of agony — but still a child of liberty — a rainbow on the darkest fold of the terrific storm!

When Rouget de l'Isle [1] in winter poverty struck from the broken strings of his crushed heart the electrifying dithyrambics of the Marseillaise, that heart was France. What his whole bleeding country felt, that single soldier felt; and with more of truth than of the pompous Louis Quatorze, it could be said of that young brave — *The kingdom it was he!*

---

[1] Joseph Rouget de l'Isle, born 1760, received a pension of 1500 francs per annum for the composition of the words of the Marseillaise. The song was first sung by the Marseilles confederates, or Girondists, in 1792. It was suppressed by the Bourbons, but came up again in 1830, and has since been one of the national hymns of France.

Money, some years ago, was offered for a
national hymn. Futility! money may buy
machinery — sometimes in the form of men —
but inspiration, never![1]

The very sentiment of a national song is the
grand idea of the liberty-loving people — the
words are from the burning heart of the nation
itself — God speaking through it — they are
the synthetic expression of the politics of the
nation — they are the golden censer that en-
shrines the hopes of the nation. They hence
become the living tongue of the nation, the
leader of the nation, the guardian angel of the
nation.

From the very spirit then in which they are
conceived; from the very truths which they
enunciate, as well as from the associations which
they awaken, they become eloquent preachers
in every crusade against oppression — engines
mightier than the rifled cannon — because behind the rifle cannon for defending liberty.

As they spring, electric flashes, from the
heart of a nation, so are they in turn winged

[1] In the spring of 1861, a committee of gentlemen of New
York offered the sum of $500 for the best national hymn

with such power to reenkindle the heart of a
nation, and while true music, always of itself
awakens thoughts of the invisible, the spiritual
and the grand, so being allied to words that
breathe as heard in our great national anthems—
it in union aids to swell the tide of patriotic
emotion till it surges over the barriers to human
progress and leaves the constellated stars of freedom shining in unclouded radiance over us.

III. But Little Music in the Old Colonial Times.

1. I have intimated that a great national
song is the offspring of a great national emotion;
hence we could hardly look for any remarkable
patriotic hymn in this country anterior to the
revolution.

Our forefathers were too busy to be musical;
too sedate to listen to secular songs; too dis-

---

adapted to the then existing condition of the country. Something like twelve hundred competitors presented lyrical
pieces, but not one of them was deemed of sufficient merit
to claim the prize.

3

tinct in race and government to be inspired by
the same living, fostering, patriotic thought.
God was their commander; the songs they sang
were in the main addressed to him; and, if
sometimes a secular ditty was heard to break
the dull monotony of the spinning wheel of a
winter's evening, it was in some mournful minor
key, as

> "My name was Robert Kidd [1]
> And so wickedly I did ;
> God's laws I did forbid
> As I sailed, as I sailed."

or

> Lord Bateman, he was a noble lord,
> A lord of high degree.

or of the *Cruel Barbara Allen*.[2]

Such wild songs as the *Maypole of Merrie
Mount; Begone dull Care; Betty Martin* (from
O! mihi beati Martini) ;

> Old Adam was caused to slumber,
> A rib taken out of his side ;

being heard only in those Bacchanalian revels

---

[1] Executed May 9th, 1701. See Cooper's *History of the
Navy*, vol. I, p. 25.

[2] This is an ancient Scottish ballad inserted in Allan
Ramsay's *Tea Table Miscellany*. Sir W. Scott's *Remarks
on Popular Poetry*.

which the bar-room of colonial times would sometimes witness.

Even the revolution itself did not produce any very creditable patriotic song. The famous semi-sacred psalms of *Chester* and *Columbia*, by that famous Boston tanner and musician, William Billings,[1] over whose sign-board .some one hung a couple of contending cats to indicate the music which he made, were the favorite camp songs of that day.

2. *Gen. James Wolfe's Song.*

The earliest American soldier-song which became broadly popular is said to have emanated from the fertile fancy of Gen. James Wolfe, in 1759.

As the boat of this gallant soldier was gliding over the silent tide of the St. Lawrence on

---

[1] Born October 7, 1746, and died in Boston, September 26, 1800. He published six different works on psalmody, embracing many pieces of his own composition. The spirit of the revolution appears in many of his verses, and some of his psalm tunes were frequently played on the fife and drum in the revolutionary army. The words to *Chester* which were written by himself, are :

> Let tyrants shake their iron rod,
>   And slavery clank her galling chains;
> We'll fear them not — we trust in God;
>   New England's God forever reigns.

the eve of that battle which gave him death and glory, he repeated in a low wailing tone, that celebrated, and to him prophetic strain of Gray :

> The boast of heraldry, the pomp of power,
>   And all that beauty, all that wealth ere gave,
> Await alike the inevitable hour ;
>   The paths of glory lead but to the grave.

and then under the inspiration of the hour and yet as if in contrast to the thought — a sparkle of light upon the darkling wave — he sang :

> How stands the glass around ! [1]
> For shame ye take no care, my boys ;
> How stands the glass around !
> Let mirth and wine abound
> The trumpet sounds,
> The colors, they are flying, boys.

which was sung in the messes of officers and squads of soldiers in both armies through the revolution, and which is still a popular military song.

The death of Wolfe created an intense sensation both in England and America, and a few

---

[1] The idea is from *Why Soldiers, why*, in the *Patron*, 1729. *How stands the glass around*, first appeared in William Shield's *Siege of Gibraltar*, 1775. It is questionable whether Wolfe composed the song. See Chappell's *Popular Music of the Olden Times*, vol. II, p. 689.

years afterwards the notorious Thomas Paine, author of the *Age of Reason*, wrote his celebrated ode in memory of the lamented hero. It is a beautiful specimen of English anapestic verse; graceful in rhythm and melody, yet a little over strained in sentiment. The music is the fine old plaintive English air called *The Gods of the Greeks*, and is well adapted to the words.

This song continued popular long after the revolution, and nothing brings my dear old father's features more distinctly to my mind than the words of the closing stanza, which his noble tenor voice would render so effectively as to leave our young eyes brimming full of patriotic tears![1]   " To the plains of Quebec " — it is the death angel who speaks :

" To the plains of Quebec with the orders I flew ;
   He begged for a moment's delay ;
He cried ' O forbear ! let me victory hear
   And then thy commands I'll obey ! '
With a darksome thick film I encompassed his eye
   And bore him away in an urn,
Lest the fondness he bore for his own native shore,
   Should induce him again to return."

---

[1] " The melody of youthful days
Which steals the trembling tear of speechless praise."

Mr. Paine afterwards wrote in the same graceful measure and to the same beautiful tune, his well known *Liberty Tree :*

> " In the chariot of light from the regions of day
> 　　The goddess of Liberty came ;
> Ten thousand celestials directed her way,
> 　　And hither conducted the dame.
> A fair budding branch from the gardens above,
> 　　Where millions with millions agree,
> She brought in her hand as a pledge of her love,
> 　　And the plant she named *Liberty tree."*

which had influence in fanning the flame of patriotism in the days of yore.

.

IV. Music of the Revolution, Yankee Doodle.

It were quite easy to trace the progress and to write the history of the American revolution itself, from this period to its eventful close, by the patriotic songs which were written in commemoration of the scenes as they transpired ; and these songs, though homely in style and sentiment, sung in the camps of the soldiers, were undoubtedly as effective in inspiring and keeping alive the spirit of patriotism as the voices of Adams, Otis, and of Henry, in the forum. I can, however, refer only to one of the most prominent of these songs. Its music touched the heart of every patriot soldier then; and rings with a fresh power through every patriotic bosom still. It bears the quaint but spirit-stirring name of *Yankee Doodle!*

This is indeed a free and easy, queer and comical, good-for-nothing, rolicksome sort of a tune; with a dash of a saucy, mind-your-own-business in it; a drole, as a Frenchman, and a rigmarole, as an Englishman, would be like to call it; and yet it is fairly naturalized; and this by one of the most intelligent nations in the world; which unmistakeably implies, what I most honestly believe, that the tune has real "snap and ring and ginger" in it; and though of humble origin, is worthy of a brief biography. The term Yankee is evidently a corruption of the word *English* or of the French, *Anglais,*[1] as

---

[1] "Le mot Yankee," says M Philarète Chasles, *Revue des Deux Mondes*, May 15, 1850," n'est autre que le mot *English* transformé par la pronouciation défectueuse des indige-

imperfectly and gutturally spoken by the Indians and the real meaning of *Yankee Doodle*
would therefore be *English simpleton.*

The tune, it is very well known, is a daughter
of the regiment — coming to us by adoption.
Its parentage is involved in great obscurity;
many cities, as in case of Homer, claiming it.
Some consider it an old vintage song of France;
the Spaniards think their vales have echoed to
its notes in early days;[1] the Magyars, with
Louis Kossuth, recognize in it one of their old
national dances. England entertains some sha-

nes du Massachusetts; *Yenghis, Yanghis, Yankies.* Les
Anglais quand ils se moquent des *Yankies*, se moquent
d'eux-memes."

And so the Rev. James C. Richmond rightly sings:

> " At Yankies, John, beware to laugh;
> Against yourself you joke;
> For Yenghees, English, is but half
> By Indian natives spoke."

[1] The following note is from a secretary of legation at
Madrid:

MADRID, June 3, 1858.

My Dear Sir: The tune *Yankee Doodle*, from the first
of my showing it here, has been acknowledged by persons
acquainted with music to bear a strong resemblance to the
popular airs of Biscay; and yesterday, a professor from the
north recognized it as being much like the ancient sword
dance played on solemn occasions by the people of San Se-
bastian. He says the tune varies in those provinces, and

dowy traditions of its birth before the times of Cromwell; and the Dutchman claims it as a low country song of tithes and bonnyclabber; giving, it is said, as the original words:

> " Yanker didel, doodel, down;
> Didel, dudel, lanter,
> Yanke viver, voover vown
> Botermilk and tather." [tithes]

But whatever may have been its origin, this child of the regiment, so far as I can learn, first appeared in America on the banks of the Hud-

---

proposes in a couple of months to give me the changes as they are to be found in their different towns, that the matter may be judged of and fairly understood. Our national air certainly has its origin in the music of the free Pyrenees; the first strains are identically those of the heroic *Danza Esparta*, as it was played to me, of brave old Biscay.

Very truly yours,
BUCKINGHAM SMITH.

The origin of the word *Yankee* has greatly perplexed the etymologists; yet that given in the text is by far the most probable. Anbury, in his *Travels through the Interior of North America*, vol. II, p. 46, says it is derived from a Cherokee word, *eankke*, which means coward and slave. See *Drake's Book of the Indians*, book I, p. 23. Others deduce it from the old Scotch word *Yankie*, a sharp, clever woman. A writer in the *Boston Weekly Magazine*, for January 29, 1803, says it is from *Yankau*, an Indian word for con-

4

son, in June, 1755 ;[1] and was introduced into
the American camp by one mischievous Dr.
Richard Shuckburgh[2] of the British army in
this amusing way.   Our colonial companies
under Gov. William Shirley, then encamped
on the left of the British army, meanly
disciplined and still more meanly clad; some
in long tailed blue coats, some in long-tailed
black coats, some in no coats at all, heads
shorn — heads unshorn, and marching after
music quite two centuries old, incurred, of
course, the ridicule of their fashionable trans-
atlantic allies.

---

queror ; but most writers now agree with Mr. Heckewelder,
that it,is a corruption of the word *Anglais*, or *English*, made
by the Indians in pronouncing it.

Yengees, says Mrs. Child, in *Hobomok*, p. 39, is " The
Indian term for English from which *Yankee* is probably
derived."

Dr. Trumbull says, in a note to one of his poems,
" The Indians, in attempting to utter the word *English*,
with their broad, guttural accent, gave it a sound which
would be nearly represented in this way; *Younghees* —
[Yankees]."

[1] For the history of this national air, see N. H. Carter's
article in *Moore's Historical Miscellany*, vol. III, p. 217.

[2] Richard Shuckburg was appointed secretary of Indian
affairs by Sir William Johnson, in 1760. *Documentary
History of New York*, II, 460.

To keep the sport along, this naughty Dr. Shuckburgh, wit, fiddler, surgeon as he was, tells the Americans that their music is too comical, and that he will get up a tune for them in modern style, and so he gives *Yankee Doodle!* " Mighty fine ! " the raw recruits cry out. It strikes at once the strong chord in the American heart, and is heard immediately, and nothing else is heard throughout the camp — the colonies.

It became our battle march[1] in the revolution, and although the British gave it us, June, 1755, we gave it back to them, June, 1775, with compound interest. We then baptized the bantling in the blood of heroes ; placed upon it the fair name of FREEDOM, rocked it in old Faneuil Hall, and took it home to live with us forever.

By a strong poetic license, Geo. P. Morris makes the adoption of *Yankee Doodle* date back only to the destruction of tea in Boston harbor;

[1] " While every rebel fife in play
To Yankee Doodle tuned its lay,
And like the music of the spheres,
Mellifluous soothed their vanquished ears."
M' Fingal, Canto VI.

yet well he writes in the bright spirit of the tune, and to the tune itself.

> " A long war then they had, in which
> John was at last defeated ;
> And *Yankee Doodle* was the march,
> To which their troops retreated.
>
> ' Cute Jonathan, to see them fly,
> Could not restrain his laughter ;
> ' That tune,' said he, ' suits to a T,
> I'll sing it ever after,' "

And so he still keeps singing it — and so the foe still flies before it.

The brigade under Lord Percy played *Yankee Doodle* in contempt of the Americans as they moved on Lexington[1]—they played another tune returning — but still they sang it through the streets of Boston to such words as :

> " Yankee Doodle came to town,
> For to buy a firelock ;
> We will tar and feather him,
> And so we will John Hancock."

Although the British gave us *Yankee Doodle* as a joke, I think we fully paid them back in

---

[1] In his very able account of the battle of Lexington, the Hon. Charles Hudson says : " Percy marched out through Roxbury, to the tune of *Yankee Doodle.*" See *History of Lexington*, p. 197 – 8.

their own coin for it, in the merry songs which it inspired at their expense before the revolution ended.

The most remarkable of these was written by Francis Hopkinson, Esquire,[1] author of *General Washington's March*, and most appropriately called the *Battle of the Kegs*.

In 1777, a genuine Yankee, by the name of David Bushnell, born in Saybrook, undertook to blow up the British fleet, then lying at Philadelphia, by a sort of a gim-crack which he called his *submarine torpedo;* which nonsensical instrument, looked like a mud tortoise with a man astride his back; and was just about as slow in movement.

Failing in this, he then prepares a quantity of wooden kegs, or porpoises; fills them with some kind of explosive powder; arranges them with a spring lock so as to go off when coming

---

[1] Son of Judge Thomas Hopkinson, who assisted Dr. Franklin in his electrical discoveries. He was born at Philadelphia, in 1737, and died on the 8th of May, 1791. " His head is not bigger than a large apple," writes John Adams to his wife in 1776, " yet he is genteel, well-bred and very social." He married the accomplished Miss Ann Borden, of Bordentown, New Jersey, in 1767.

in contact with a solid body ; and sends them
floating down the Delaware river among the
vessels of the British fleet.   One of these black-
heads bumping against some object in the river,
happens to explode, and the British soldiers
seeing the stream alive with them, and sup-
posing each to contain a living Yankee, are
most wofully alarmed and open a general fire,
which is of course returned by a general
fizzle, from Bushnell's battery.   This engage-
ment, fitly named *The Battle of the Kegs*,
afforded the facile pen of Hopkinson, a theme
for the wittiest ballad of the revolution.   Hear
for example, the cry of the affrighted British
sailors :

> " These kegs, I'm told, the rebels hold,
>   Packed up like pickled herring ;
> And they're come down to attack the town,
>   In this new way of ferrying ! "

and when was British valor ever better eulo-
gized than in the closing stanzas :

> " From morn to night these men of might
>   Displayed amazing courage ;
> And when the sun was fairly down,
>   Retired to sup their porridge.   ˎ

A hundred men with each a pen
Or more, upon my word, sir,
It is most true, would be too few
Their valor to record, sir.

Such feats did they perform that day,
Against these wicked kegs, sir ;
That years to come, if they get home,
They'll make their boast and brags, sir."

God Save King George, began the revolution, Yorktown and *Yankee Doodle* — for it was played at the surrender of Cornwallis[1] — ended it; and so on its great march rejoicing, this queer, old, plucky, continental, saltpetre, and brimstone tune, has been outsoldiering its enemies, and continues to outsoldier them till our dear old striped bunting now streams from every flag-staff in the land again !

, Men laugh at *Yankee Doodle,* yet they love it; they find all manner of fault with it, as with the romping, reckless, hoyden girl of the family; and yet they make the most of it. The world indeed has no tune like it.

Over the River to Charlie ; Ça ira, à la Lanterne, les Aristocrats ; St. Patrick's Day in the

---

[1] See *John F. Watson's Annals of Philadelphia,* vol. II, p. 333.

Morning, are as much inferior to it as Charles
the Pretender, or Maximilian Robespierre, or the
tutelary saint of Ireland were to Washington.
"Independence now, and independence forever,"
rings in every note of it; and we never feel half
so much like the very '76 itself, as when we
hear it rolling. "For a change," once said a *bon
vivant,* "let me have water, but for a steady
drink, Old Cogniac!" For a change, I also say,
let me have brass and Verdi; but for steady
martial music, fife and drum and *Yankee Doodle.*
⬇ It is a perfectly democratic tune — alike for
lofty and for lowly. This, the young country
fiddler, seated on a trunk among the wasps and
cobwebs of the attic, first learns to scrape out
upon his squeaking catgut. On this the grand
maestro weaves his wild fantasia and calls it
"Opus number 42." To this the raw recruit
first learns to "mark the time" upon the muster
field. To this the young collegian writes his
Latin thesis:

"Nunc rite gratulandum est;
Nec abstinendum joco;
Peractis binis sæculis
Desipitur in loco!"

Its music cheers the fisherman on the lonely coast of Labrador; it rises mid the wildest acclamations when the stately 74 flings out her pennon of the stripes and stars in the enchanting Bay of Naples. This is the *pas de charge* of our victorious troops advancing on the hostile legions; the last strain that greets the soldier's ear before he wakens to the rapturous songs of the celestial armies.

It has done something for the people, and the people love it. It is the blood of their political life, and you might as well attempt to rob them of Bunker Hill, or of the Stars and Stripes themselves, as of this dear old clinking, clattering, right about face, defiant battle march!

V. SONGS AT THE CLOSE OF THE LAST CENTURY, ROBERT PAINE'S ADAMS AND LIBERTY, ETC.

The year 1798 brought forth three celebrated national songs. Our country, then steering itself between the political Sylla and Charybdis of France and England, was expecting to be

5

dashed upon the rocks on one side or the other.
The caldron of party strife was seething hotly;
democrats and federalists were roused to fury
by the contending factions in the hostile govern-
ments of Europe, so that the calm voice of
Washington and these immortal songs seem,
alone, to have saved us from political destruction.   They came, according to a law to which
I have referred, out of the bosom of the storm;
and they in turn most powerfully conspired to
quell the storm.

Two of them were written by sons of signers
of the Declaration of Independence.

Robert Treat Paine, born in Taunton, Massachusetts, Dec. 9, 1773, was christened by, to
him, the unfortunate name of Thomas, which
he subsequently had changed to Robert because,
as he observed, in allusion to the author of the
Age of Reason, " he had no *Christian* name."

Vain, fanciful, indolent, he was petted and
spoiled in college, and then married a beautiful
play-actress, for which his father foolishly for-
bade him access to his house.   He subsequently
gave himself up to poetry, wine and theatricals,
any one of which is enough to ruin a man.

He inherited, however, from his honored sire, the spirit of patriotism, and at the age of twenty-five produced his celebrated song *Adams and Liberty*, which rang like an angel's trumpet through the land, and for which he received seven hundred dollars cash, and immortality.[1] It opens grandly thus:

" Ye sons of Columbia who bravely have fought
  For those rights which unstained from your sires had descended,
May you long taste the blessings your valor has bought,
  And your sons reap the soil which your fathers defended;
      'Mid the reign of mild peace
      May your nation increase,
    With the glory of Rome and the wisdom of Greece;
And ne'er shall the sons of Columbia be slaves,
While the earth bears a plant or the sea rolls its waves."

The eighth stanza was written impromptu, under a double pressure, and is of course the best. Many a verse has been inspired by wine, but this was written for the want of it.

---

[1] He died Nov. 13th, 1811, and his works were published in one volume by Charles Prentiss in 1812. He is the author of *Rise Columbia*, 1794, and other patriotic songs. Referring to him, one of his biographers observes: " he was an electric battery charged; if you touched him, the sparks flew."

Dining with his friend, Major Benjamin Russell, of the *Centinel*, one day, Paine was reminded that his lyric was imperfect, inasmuch as the name of Washington was omitted; and his host declared he should not taste a drop of wine until he had produced another stanza.

The bibacious poet sees the glasses sparkling on the board, and calling for a pen immediately writes as from the innermost shrine of his glowing heart:

" Should the tempest of war overshadow our land,
   Its bolts would ne'er rend Freedom's temple asunder,
For unmoved at its portals would Washington stand,
   And repulse with his breast the assaults of the thunder;
      His sword from the sleep
      Of its scabbard would leap,
   And conduct with its point every flash to the deep;
And ne'er shall the sons of Columbia be slaves,
While the earth bears a plant or the sea rolls its waves."

JOSEPH HOPKINSON'S HAIL COLUMBIA.

The same year, 1798, when war with France appeared inevitable — indeed had actually begun — gave birth to another liberty hymn, conceived in the very loftiest style of patriotic devotion — enshrining, as it were, the spirit of freedom and the glory of the illustrious sage of Mount Vernon about to ascend to heaven, and passing them over embalmed in music to the incoming century.

The field music of the revolution consisted mainly of *Yankee Doodle; On the Road to Boston; Rural Felicity; My Dog and Gun*, and *Washington's March;*[1] but on the occasion of Washington's first attendance at the theatre in New York, 1789, a German by the name of Feyles composed a tune to take the place of *Washington's March*, christening it with the name *President's March*.

It soon became a favorite, and on a certain Monday evening in the summer of 1798, an indifferent singer by the name of Fox, belonging to the Philadelphia theatre, was about to take his benefit.

Saturday morning came; not a ticket had been sold and a "beggarly account of empty boxes" was before him, when a good thought struck his brain.

---

[1] Composed in G, by the Hon. Francis Hopkinson. See *Historical Magazine* for January, 1859.

Congress was in session; political strife exciting; the storm of war was lowering, and a patriotic song, especially if he could get one written to Feyles's President's March, would save him.

He knew a clever young lawyer, once his schoolmate, and son of the witty author of the *Battle of the Kegs.* His name was Joseph Hopkinson[*]— name famous. then in law and literature, but still more famous now.

The poetic lawyer pities his friend Fox, bids him call again on Sunday afternoon, and then he gives him——O the prize that glides into the poor player's fingers, and through those fingers into this great nation — he gives him —

"Hail Columbia, happy land,
Hail ye heroes, heaven-born band,
Who fought and bled in freedom's cause,
And when the storm of war was gone
Enjoyed the peace your valor won;

---

[1] Son of Francis and Mary (Borden) Hopkinson, and born in Philadelphia, Nov. 12, 1770; graduated at the University of Pennsylvania, and was counsel for Dr. Rush in his suit against the celebrated William Cobbett. Congressman from 1815 to 1819, and appointed judge in 1828. He was president of the Philadelphia Academy of Fine Arts, and died, highly respected, Jan. 15, 1842.

> Let independence be your boast;
> Ever mindful what it cost;
> Ever grateful for the prize,
> Let its altar reach the skies.
> Firm, united let us be,
> Rallying round our liberty;
> As a band of brothers joined,
> Peace and safety we shall find."

And then :

> "Immortal patriots rise once more,
> Defend your rights, defend your shore."

And still more grand it rolls along to the pealing climax :

> " Sound, sound the trump of fame;
> Let Washington's great name
> Ring through the world with loud applause."

Nine times the audience call for it, and then rising altogether join with rapturous tongues in the full chorus.

It filled the theatre — it fired the national heart — it raised the dome of patriotism far above the minarets of faction, and bound us with the bands of faith and probity in political union.

It is, you will observe, a purely patriotic hymn. It makes no reference to France or

England, democrat or federalist. It therefore
pleased alike each party. Every word is
instinct with freedom. It is a clarion peal,
each note of it, from the *avant couriers* of our
liberty; and as it electrified the hearts of
Washington, Hamilton, Jefferson, McHenry,
then, so its great glowing thoughts make our
hearts leap exultingly to-day.

Jefferson gave us the Declaration of Independence; Hamilton gave us the Constitution;
Washington gave us his Farewell Address —
was the benefaction less when Hopkinson gave
us *Hail Columbia?* [1]

SUMNER'S ODE ON SCIENCE.

I am inclined to believe the citizens of Taunton are not remarkably felicitous in respect to
the names of their children. We have seen it

[1] In the original arrangement of this celebrated song,
which lies before me, it is styled, " The favorite new Federal
Song adapted to the President's March : sung by Mr. Fox,
written by J. Hopkinson, Esq." The music is in the key
of C. For the author's own account of the composition, see
Moore's *Encyclopedia of Music*, article " Hail Columbia."

in the singular mistake of ushering one of them
into the world under the unchristian title of
Thomas Paine, and a clerical friend of ours
recently administered the holy rite of baptism
in one of the churches of that thriving town to
a little love pledge under the sweet name of
Mary, when the father terrified flew up to him,
in face of the assembly, saying: "We have one
Mary in the family already — what a sad mistake — can you not *unbaptize* her?" And many
a year ago a father gave his little son the
unmerciful prænomen of *Jazaniah* to bear along
with him through this gainsaying world; but
Jazaniah Sumner came to be a noble hearted,
unpretending, patriotic man; a deacon of the
church, who loved his country more than his
political party, and when in 1798 the excellent
Mr. Simeon Daggett was preparing the young
gentlemen and ladies for the fiftieth annual
examination of the Taunton Academy, the good
deacon, Jazaniah Sumner, was inditing a song,
both words and music, to be sung on the occasion. Though political in its bearing, he gave
it the name of *Ode on Science,* and this, so far
as I can learn, is the first good patriotic song

6

whose music and whose words were both composed by an American. The author's letter[1]
to Mr. Daggett, with the autograph of the
original music lies before me as I write. The
words are strictly national and patriotic:

I.

"The morning sun shines from the east
And spreads his glories to the west,
All nations with his beams are blest
    Where'er his radiant light appears;
So Science spreads her lucid ray
O'er lands that long in darkness lay:
She visits fair Columbia
    And sets her sons among the stars."

II.

"Fair Freedom her attendant waits
To bless the portals of her gates,
To crown the young and rising states,
    With laurels of immortal day.
The British yoke, the Gallic chain,
Was urged upon our sons in vain;
All haughty tyrants we disdain,
    And shout — 'Long live America.' "

The author strikes at France and England
alike, exalting our own land in glory between

---

[1] *Jazaniah Sumner's Letter to Mr. Simeon Daggett,
Preceptor of Taunton Academy.*

SIR : While I was anticipating the pleasing satisfaction
of a respectable audience who will probably attend on the
day of exhibition, I was anxious that we on our part might

them, and when on a certain occasion the federalists in that part of Taunton, since called Raynham, inserted the word *Jacobins* instead of *tyrants* in the chorus and thundered out:

> " All haughty Jacobins we disdain,
> And shout ' Long live America.' "

a terrific storm of indignation burst forth from the Jeffersonian wing of the house and the meeting broke up in confusion. Though the words of this song are not remarkably poetical, the music is as original and peculiar as Timothy Swan's old tune of *China*. The chorus comes out in fine relief to the plaintiveness of the quar-

---

add something to the novelty of the day. In searching our church music I could find nothing suitable which was the cause of my attempting this small piece of music, together with the lines. It will be a sufficient apology for me to say that I have no pretensions to a poetical genius, nor have I trod the flowery path of science, but hope my attempt may emulate some superior genius who may offer something more worthy your acceptance.

Such as it is it is humbly dedicated to you, sir (together with my sincere wishes that you may long preside over the useful institution in this place, and have the satisfaction to see your labors crown'd with success), by your most obedient servant,
JAZANIAH SUMNER.

Taunton, April 3, 1798.
    To Mr. Simeon Daggett.

tette with the ring of a war trumpet. Had
the tune commenced, as the *Gods of the Greeks*,
upon a lower note, it would have been more
popular still. The first step is unfortunately
the longest one, and that too often prevents the
people from taking any step at all; but the tune
is national, our first national patriotic tune; it
performed good service in its day, and hence in
memory of the times gone by we love to sing it
and to speak the name of Jazaniah Sumner still.

✗

VI. The Early Songs of this Present Century.

Of the patriotic songs which appeared in the
early part of this century and even to the war
of 1812, none perhaps were more popular than
Mrs. Susanna Rowson's spirited *America, Com-
merce and Freedom;* and *Jefferson and Liberty,*
written to an old Irish air in 1801. Our ladies
used to sing at that period Thomas Campbell's
Exiles of Erin; Since then I'm Doomed, from the
Spoiled Child; Tell me, babbling Echo, and
Bidwell's *Friendship;* our seamen, *Black Eyed
Susan,* and Charles Dibdin's beautiful *Tom Bow-*

line; our young sentimentalists, Gen. John Burgoyne's *Encompassed in an Angel's Frame,* and Sterne's *Maria;* while our old men in their social interviews made the welkin ring with *Hail Columbia, Adams and Liberty,* and Sumner's *Ode on Science,* bringing in as interludes, it might be, the *Soldier's Return;* the *Bright Rosy Morning; Life let us Cherish; Begone dull Care,* and intermingling now and then the minor strains of the old *Indian Death Song :*[1]

" The sun sets at night and the stars shun the day."

Gilderoy; Wife, Children and Friends ;[2] Major Andre's *Lament,* and Oswald's sorrow-breathing *Roslin Castle.*[3]

---

[1] The words of this once popular song, sometimes ascribed to Philip Freneau, were written by Mrs. John Hunter, a sister of Sir Everard Home. " The idea was suggested several years ago," says the author, "by hearing a gentleman who had resided many years ago in America among the tribe called the Cherokees, sing a wild air which he assured me it was customary for those people to chant with a barbarous jargon, implying contempt of their enemies in the moments of torture and death." See Duyckinck's *Cyc. of Am. Lit.,* vol. I, p. 341.

[2] By the Hon. William R. Spencer, 1770–1834.—*Cyc. Eng. Lit.,* II, 421.

[3] " Its no a Scots tune, but it passes for one. Oswald

But the impressment of seamen, the embargo and Mr. Madison's war that followed, threw the country into another exigence, and by the law that the bruised flower yields the sweetest perfume, another national lyric, the brightest of the constellation, sprang from it to breathe fresh inspiration into every loyal heart. The war had come down to its darkest hour, and while in commemoration of our naval victories inferior hands were striking out such clever songs as *Our Flag is there,* and while some in livelier mood were giving us the *Jolly Enterprise and Boxer,* and, to the tune of *Eveline's Bower,*

> " I often have been told,
> That the British seamen bold,
> Could beat the tars of France neat and handy, O."

One solitary eye in fine frenzy rolling, caught a spark of true Promethean fire and conferred a royal benefaction on his native land.

---

made it himsell, I reckon. He has cheated mony ane, but he canna cheat Wandering Willie. He then played your favorite air of *Roslin Castle* with a number of beautiful variations."—*Red Gauntlet,* p. 31.

Francis Scott Key's Star Spangled Banner.

In the month of August, 1814, the country hung upon the verge of ruin. Our army led by Dearborn, Hull and Winder was diminishing under a succession of deplorable reverses. The democrats and federalists were burning with political rancor; our financial credit had run down to zero, and our currency was such that it required a dollar to buy a single yard of cotton cambric cloth. In the midst of this general gloom Lord George Cockburn enters the Chesapeake with a fleet of 20 sail, and makes a quick advance on Washington.

At Bladensburg, Md., the British army, 4,000 veterans, under Major Robert Ross, encounters Gen. William H. Winder, who, fighting feebly, soon sets out on what is called the Bladensburg races, for the woods.

Cockburn enters Washington — the capitol — ascends into the speaker's chair and puts the question to his soldiers : " Shall this harbor of Yankee democracy be burned ? " " Yes ! yes ! " cry out a thousand voices, and, in a little, flames are rising over all the city, and the capital is in ruins.

Cockburn now turns his course on Baltimore, defended by 10,000 men and Fort M'Henry. Ross lands his troops below the city and commences marching on it; while the fleet, increased to forty sail, prepares for the bombardment of the fort.

Meantime a little vessel guided by a brave young man, and bearing a white flag of truce, shoots out from underneath the guns of Fort M'Henry, and glides like a bird down the broad bay directly to the flag ship of the British squadron.

That man is Francis Scott Key.[1] He goes to intercede for the deliverance of his dear old friend Dr. Beanes, who had been taken prisoner at the *races.*

Cockburn detains him.

The squadron, forming a vast semicircle, moves, like a vulture with its talons spread,

---

[1] Francis Scott Key, son of John Ross Key, an officer in the revolutionary army, was born Aug. 1, 1779, and died Jan. 11, 1843, leaving a numerous family. One of his sons was shot in a duel by John Sherburne of Portsmouth, N. H., and another, Philip Barton Key, was killed at Washington by Daniel E. Sickles on Sunday, Feb. 27, 1859.

as if to grasp and crush at one fell swoop the silent fort.

Key's boat is kept astern of the flag ship of the admiral, himself a prisoner in it, and from this point he hears above the booming of the floods the steady cannonading on the shore.

From this point he sees the lingering sunbeams of the 13th of September fade away beneath the forests on the west; he sees the heavy clouds come rolling over the dark waters of the bay, and a dim twinkling light from the low promontory of the Fort M'Henry, now the slender pivot on which our national destiny is turning.

From that frail skiff, moored to the tall admiral he marks the mighty preparations for the onset — the clearing of the decks, the ranging of the guns, the furling of the canvas.

And now — ah, look, the long and curved line of brazen lips are spouting forth the fiery streams of death, directed to one common centre — Fort M'Henry.

Ah, look! The globes of fire cast lurid gleams upon the inky clouds above, the waves are flashing in the flames below.

7

Ah look! A torrent hissing from the fort comes crashing back into the ships; and now sheets of flame and bursting shells, and red hot shot, and bugle notes and falling masts, and streams of gore and battle agony — the consternation and the havoc and the din of direful war. You can see it, tell it I cannot.

All through the thundering crash of that long, horrid night,[1] the prisoner stands in his light skiff, intently gazing on the rolling floods of fire — heaven, earth, and sea in one wild blaze; a leaf—himself and country—shaken by the tempest to the very verge of doom.

---

[1] Sixteen hundred bombs by old Cockburn's command,
At our fort were discharged by his famed sons of plunder,
While unmoved stood brave Armistead's well chosen band,
Sending back their full change in red hot Yankee thunder.
Battle of North Point.

The bombardment began at daylight on the 13th inst., and continued till the morning of the 14th, about twenty-five hours. The night was dark and stormy, with thunder and lightning. Four hundred shells exploded within the fort, and yet only four of our men were killed. See *The Late War* by William James, vol. II, p. 307; also *Notices of the War of* 1812, by John Armstrong, vol. II, p. 136. In his *History of Maryland*, John M'Sherry says, vol. II, p. 343, the bombardment began on the evening of the 13th of September, which is evidently a mistake.

But lo! the fire balls cease to flame across the bay; the roar of the terrific conflict is subsiding, and now all is dark and still again.

Has the fort M'Henry struck her flag?

Oh, what an hour of agony!

With straining eyes Key waits and watches for the first gray beam of breaking day — even as the saint for the first gleams of immortality.

But now the clouds roll by, the dawn is trembling on the headlands, the mist is clearing, and there, just rising dimly from the ramparts through the gray vail of the morning Key discerns — oh, thrilling as the vision of an angel from the gates of Eden — Key discerns the dear old stripes and stars still waving!

Snatching an old letter from his pocket, he lays it on a barrel-head, and while the flag is in his eye, the fiery tides of liberty coursing through his soul, he writes:

I.

"O! say can you see by the dawn's early light,
What so proudly we hailed at the twilight's last gleaming;
Whose broad stripes and bright stars through the perilous fight,
O'er the ramparts we watched were so gallantly streaming;
And the rocket's red glare, the bombs bursting in air,
Gave proof through the night that our flag was still there.
O say! does the star-spangled banner still wave, ·
O'er the land of the free and the home of the brave!"

II.

" On the shore dimly seen through the mist of the deep,
  Where the foe's haughty host in dread silence reposes,
What is that which the breeze o'er the towering steep,
  As it fitfully blows, half conceals, half discloses ?
Now it catches the gleam of the morning's first beam,
In full glory reflected, now it shines on the stream ;
'Tis the star-spangled banner, O ! long may it wave,
O'er the land of the free and the home of the brave."

III.

" O thus be it ever when freemen shall stand,
  Between their loved homes and war's desolation ;
Blessed with victory and peace, may the heaven-rescued land,
  Praise the power that hath made and preserved us a nation.
Then conquer we must, when our cause it is just,
And this be our motto — ' In God is our trust.'
And the star-spangled banner in triumph shall wave,
O'er the land of the free and the home of the brave." [1]

Cockburn soon left the bay; God save the king — the country !

The music of the *Star Spangled Banner* was composed by Dr. Samuel Arnold,[2] Oxford, England, for the old hunting song *Anacreon in Heaven.*

[1] These words were originally published in the Baltimore *Patriot* on the 20th of September, 1814, under the title cf *The Defence of Fort McHenry.*

[2] Dr. Samuel Arnold [1739–1802], author of *The Maid of the Mill,* and the oratorios of *The Prodigal Son, Abimelech, The Curse of Saul,* and *The Resurrection ;*

It is, I dare maintain in opposition to the critics, original, elevated, soul-inspiring and most admirably suited for a national anthem.

It commences on a key so low that all may join in it.

It has unity of idea. The melodic parts most naturally succeed each other, and if I may so speak, are logically conjoined and bound together. It consists of solo, duett and chorus, and thus in unity presents variety. It is bold, warlike, and majestic; stirring the profoundest emotions of the soul, and echoing through its deepest chambers something of the prospective grandeur of a mighty nation tramping towards the loftiest heights of intellectual dominion.[1]

------

was organist and composer to his majesty's chapel at St. James's, and published a splendid edition of the works of the immortal George F. Handel in 1786. He also published four volumes of cathedral music.

[1] The effect of this national air as sung by ten thousand voices at the Peace Festival in Boston, June 15, 1869, with full orchestra, drum corps, chiming of bells, and artillery accompaniments was truly grand. At the conclusion of the last stanza the vast audience sprang up and filled with deafening cheers the Coliseum.

VII. Our Songs during the Tranquillity which Mr. Madison's War secured.

Under the cerulean skies which followed the hard contest, there frequently appeared a beautiful American song to gladden our hearts and homes, and elevate the tone of social life. As the country advanced in wealth and education, the people had more leisure and more taste for cultivating and enjoying music. The pianoforte was gradually introduced; which by its accompaniments sustained the voice and lent expression to the song. Music books were multiplied, the children in our schools were taught, and ever should be taught, to sing.

Among the popular songs of this period which may be said to have sunk deeply into the affections of the people, none is more widely known than *Home, Sweet Home,* by John Howard Payne,[1]

---

[1] Born in New York, June 9, 1792, and died in Tunis, where he was consul, in 1852. As an actor and author of several dramas he met with considerable success; but his fame will rest upon the inimitable song of *Sweet Home,* which he wrote in London for his *Clari, or the Maid of Milan,* in 1823. In giving a history of his wanderings and

who through reverse of fortune never came to taste himself the joys of that dear spot of which he sang so sweetly. It was estimated in 1832 that more than one hundred thousand copies of this favorite song had been sold by the original publisher. The music was composed by Sir

---

his trials, he once said to a friend : " How often I have been in the heart of Paris, Berlin, and London, or some other city, and heard persons singing or hand-organs playing *Sweet Home,* without having a shilling to buy myself the next meal, or a place to lay my head. The world has literally sung my song till every heart is familiar with its melody. Yet I have been a wanderer from my boyhood. My country has turned me ruthlessly from office, and in my old age I have to submit to humiliation for my bread." .

Mr. Payne wrote two additional verses to his immortal song for an American lady in London in 1833 or '4.—*Home Journal.*

To us, in despite of the absence of years,
How sweet the remembrance of home still appears,
From allurements abroad, which but flatter the eye,
The unsatisfied heart turns, and says, with a sigh,
  Home, home, sweet, sweet home !
   There's no place like home !
   There's no place like home !

Your exile is blest with all fate can bestow,
But mine has been checkered with many a woe !
Yet though different our fortunes, our thoughts are the same,
And both, as we think of Columbia, exclaim,
  Home, home, sweet, sweet home !
   There's no place like home !
   There's no place like home !

Henry R. Bishop [1782–1856], for the opera of *Clari*, which was brought out in 1823.

The Old Oaken Bucket, by Samuel Wood-worth;[1] *Woodman Spare that Tree*, and *Near the Lake there Drooped a Willow*, by George P. Morris; *God Bless our Native Land*, translated from the German by John S. Dwight, the accomplished editor of the *Journal of Music;* the *Old Arm Chair*, by Eliza Cook; the *Landing of the Pilgrims*, by George Lunt, for which Mr. T. B. White wrote the music; *A Life on the Ocean Wave*, by Epes Sargent, and

> " Rocked in the cradle of the deep
> I lay me down in peace to sleep,"

are all beautiful and well known national lyrics, which have magically touched the chords of

---

[1] Born in Scituate, Mass., Jan. 13, 1785, and died Dec. 9, 1842. He wrote also *The Hunters of Kentucky*, and other songs, for which see his *Melodies*, published in New York, 1831. The *Old Oaken Bucket* " was written in the spring or summer of 1817. The family were living at the time in Duane street. The poet came home to dinner one very warm day, having walked from his office, somewhere near the foot of Wall street. Being much heated with the exercise, he poured himself out a glass of water — New York pump water — and drank it at a draught, exclaiming, as he replaced the tumbler on the table, ' that is very refreshing, but how much more refreshing would it be to take a good

feeling, and which the people will not willingly let die. The last mentioned song is from the fertile pen of Mrs. Emma Willard,[1] one of the most celebrated female educators in America, whose fair and honored name among its gifted ones this city[2] numbers. It was written on the deep, whose mysterious spirit it so beautifully breathes, during the author's passage home from Europe in 1832. The Duke de Choiseul who

---

long draught, this warm day, from the old oaken bucket I left hanging in my father's well, at home!' Hearing this, the poet's wife, who was always a suggestive body, said, ' Selim, why wouldn't that be a pretty subject for a poem?' The poet took the hint, and under the inspiration of the moment, sat down and poured out from his very soul those beautiful lines which have immortalized the name of Woodworth."—*Home Journal.*

[1] This estimable lady is the daughter of Samuel Hart, and was born in New Berlin, Conn., in February, 1787. She commenced the Troy Seminary for Young Ladies in 1821, and is the author of several valuable educational works. She published a volume of poems in 1830. Lafayette visited her when last in America, and made her a present of a valuable diamond ring. She still resides in Troy, N. Y. As Dr. Delany said of Mrs. Cibber on her rendering of Handel's *He was despised and rejected of Men*—so may we not almost say of her who wrote:

Rocked in the cradle of the deep,

" Woman, for this, be all thy sins forgiven!"

[2] Troy, N. Y.

8

was on board the same vessel, hearing Mrs.
Willard repeat the first two lines of the lyric,
encouraged her to complete it, and then himself
composed the music for it. The air, however,
to which it is now sung was written by Mr.
J. P. Knight. When hearing some sweet voice
murmuring this ocean-song at eventide, whispering as it does of the immensity of the sea,
of the might of Him who holds it in his hand,

> " God of stillness and of motion,
> Of the rainbow and the ocean ; "

the illustrious dawn of the grand coming destiny
seems near; the soul is filled with the sublimest
aspirations, and we feel that such a song we
would be glad to have breathed over us while
the last lingering ray of life is breaking into
the immortal splendor.

VIII. Our Songs in the late War.

In the marshaling to arms for the suppression
of the late rebellion, our music came in, as you
may well suppose, to exert a most potent influence. To the stirring strains of *Yankee Doodle;*

Columbia the Gem of the Ocean, by David T. Shaw, and set to the English tune of *The Red, White and Blue; Star Spangled Banner; Hail Columbia;* and *Our Country 'tis of Thee,*[1] by Dr. S. F. Smith, the national heart thrilled anew, and as these old melodies arose from well trained bands, the braves came forth from peaceful homes to do battle in the sacred cause of liberty. Eloquence, money, did their part — but music more.

The mustering drum beat out the stories of the olden times, and stirred the hearts of men to rally round the flag; and by its enlivening roll the ranks were filled.

New songs came in to swell the tide of feeling and to throw fresh glory over the tented field.

---

[1] One of the most deservedly popular of our sacred national hymns, sung to the tune of *God save the King,* here called *America.* In a letter to me, dated Newton Centre, Mass., June 11, 1861, the accomplished and estimable author says : " The song was written at Andover during my student life there, I think in the winter of 1831–2. It was first used publicly at a Sunday School celebration of July 4th, in Park street church, Boston. I had in my possession a quantity of German song books from which I was selecting such music as pleased me, and finding *God save the King,* I proceeded to give it the ring of American republican patriotism."

John Brown's Body lies mouldering in the grave
is perhaps the most remarkable. From its quaint
expressions, mingling the mundane with the
spiritual; from the point in the highly poetical
line, "His soul's marching on"—fighting the
battles of his country still; from the simplicity
of the martial air, said to be by Philip Simonds,
which every one could sing so easily, it caught
the public ear at once; became a rallying song
of power, and called men more mightily than
the tongue of eloquence to the war.

You heard its "Hallelujah chorus" rise from
the lips of the mustering squadrons, as the song
of the cross in the times of the old crusaders.

Jefferson and Liberty, also under the name of
Raw Recruits, or *Old Glory*, had a resurrection
in the commencement of the war, and sent its
electrifying inspirations through the hearts of
millions.

In a vast assembly for obtaining men, I
heard for an hour, or more, the immortal
Everett speak in tones of most commanding
eloquence; and as he closed his soul-entrancing
periods—it was the dying music of the swan—
the bands struck up *Old Glory*, bringing the

audience in an instant to their feet, firing every heart with such enthusiasm as moved the immortal bands at Leuctra and at Marathon ; calling forth deafening thunders of acclamation, and phalanx after phalanx of men for war.

As the great drama opened and untried soldiers moved on toward the field of deadly conflict, music came in to inspire them for the bold emprise, and nerve them for the terrific onset.

On Friday evening, July 19, 1861, before the disastrous battle of Bull Run, I was lying with the Michigan 4th Regiment in front of the enemy at Fairfax Court House. The stillness of the nightfall was broken only by the report of an occasional rifle from the surrounding forest. The lights of the camp were gradually extinguished and the weary soldiers were about to spread themselves upon the broad and verdant campus of the Court House for repose. The colonel (Woodberry) said : "Come, boys, let's have a song!" The singers came around him; stretched themselves along the greensward, and the oak branches bending over them, in front of that old building where the voice of Patrick Henry had been heard in golden tones for liberty, broke forth into the glorious strains of *Hail Columbia, Star Spangled Banner*, and *Old Hundred*, making the very welkin ring with their manly voices, rising higher, and stronger, and mightier — the whole regiment now joining in — and pouring forth such a tide of music as old ocean rolls along in praise to its eternal Ruler.

I had heard something of the great masters — the glorious choruses of Bach, of Handel, Haydn, Mendelssohn — I had admired them; but not till then did I realize the sublime power of music, or so thank God for its heart-cheering strains.   I then felt that the men would fight till glory came, and I was not mistaken.

These great songs sung, the weary men, though in the front of death, sank into slumbers so profound, that the rain which soon came pattering down through the foliage of the oak trees (I remember the first drop that struck my cheek) did not awaken them.

As the tide of war rolled on, music came in as some sweet heavenly visitant, to cheer and refresh the heart of the imperiled troops.

It is not customary, as of old, for bands to play in the midst of battle. The music then is the rattling volley of musketry — the booming of the rifle cannon and the whizzing of the shot and shell ; — the bands are detailed to bear away the dead and wounded; but in some instances, when the very turning point of the day has come, as at Williamsburg — in the terrific charge at Shiloh, and in the grand advance at Gettysburg, which turned the tide of this whole nation's destiny, *Hail Columbia* and *Yankee Doodle* quickened the step of the serried columns, hastening the eventful issue.[1]

It is hard, it is tearing, smashing work to fight a battle ;—to say nothing of the intense agony, the wild phrenzy of the soul; it knocks the beauty out of the whole frame; it shakes, unhinges, doubles up the whole organization. To charge across dead men, close up and grapple in the mortal strife, is a tremendous draft on human energy. To meet the crashing

---

[1] "It was near noon, when the Zouaves, in their crimson garments, led by Colonel Duryea, charged the batteries [at Bethel] after singing *The Star Spangled Banner* in chorus."— *Atlantic Monthly*, Sept., 1862, pp. 346.

shot and shell; to fight it out with such invincible pluck as our men showed at Fredericks-
burg, Antietam, in the Wilderness, at Coal
Harbor, Petersburg, consumes the bone and
marrow of the whole constitution; but when
the hurricane is over, music comes in refresh-
ingly and most benign and comforting are its
sweet soothing tones. The spirit of the war-
worn soldier is at once revived by it; the
wounded men forget their pains beneath its
magic sway, the dead appear to sleep more
sweetly as the notes of *Hail Columbia* roll out
over them.[1]

On the bloody battle field of Shiloh, when the
fray was over, lay a captain, struck down mor-
tally by a minié ball. In his agony he strove
to reach a bloody pool of water to allay his
burning thirst. He had not strength for it.
The stars of night came out. He looked up to
the shining vault and thought of God. He
broke into a song.

---

[1] When our regimental bands played *Hail Columbia*, the
Star Spangled Banner, and other national airs after the
battle of Mill Spring, tears started to the eyes of many of
the rebel prisoners at the well remembered strains.

" When I can read my title clear,
To mansions in the skies,"

another dying soldier heard him and repeated
it — another joined the chorus, then another —
then another, until from every part of that en-
sanguined field, the music of the mansions rose
from lips of dying men to soothe the mortal
agony and antedate the empyrean harmonies.[1]

Our bands used to play in the army the beautiful airs of Mozart's *Don Giovanni,* or of *Lucretia
Borgia,* and *Il Trovatore,* with marches and quick-
steps from Chopin; from Flotow's *Martha* and
from Gonoud's *Faust;* interblended, perhaps,
with the universal favorites of the soldier;
*Annie Laurie; Her bright Eyes haunt me still;
Rosa Lee; Lilly Dale; Marching along; Sweet
Home;* and *The Girl I left behind me.*

The rebel bands which I have heard played
nearly the same tunes, always substituting,
however, the merry strains of *Dixie* for *Yankee
Doodle,* and the beautiful air, *My Maryland*
or the *Marseillaise* for the *Star Spangled Banner.*

Mighty as music is to stir the heart at home, it
has a far more potent spell upon the tented field.

---

[1] Hackett's *Memorials of the War.*

You rise, for instance, on some beautiful, clear, morning; walk along the lines of our brave army lying at rest in front of Petersburg; you hear the various bugle calls of the artillery brigades, echoing sweetly through the forest; the fife and drum of the infantry in the early drill; you catch faint sounds of *Dixie* from the intrenchments of the enemy; you hear some squad of soldiers singing rapturously " *We'll all feel gay when Johnny comes marching home;* " or *Rally round the flag, boys;* you hear another section singing the chorus of *When this cruel war is over; We are tenting to-night on the old camp ground;* or you listen of a sabbath morning in the deep wilderness, to men's voices uniting in some well known sabbath school melody, as, *I have a father in the promised land;* or to some poor wounded soldier in the hospital, murmuring in low tones,

> " O, sing to me of heaven when I am called to die,
> Sing songs of heavenly ecstacy to waft my soul on high ;"

or hold your ear to catch the slow and distant dirge, *Peace, troubled soul, whose plaintive moan,* played with muffled drums when some brave warrior is consigned by tearful comrades to his silent home, and you then begin to comprehend the power of music; the worth of music and its incalculable service in softening the horrors of war; you feel some chords thrilling in your breast that nothing on earth had ever touched before.

But there were sorrows at home as well as at the seat of war. "Partings such as crush the blood from out young hearts,"—wives and mothers weeping for the loved and stricken ones. Yet the stealing tear was often assuaged; the bitter grief consoled by the inspiring notes of national song. *We are marching to the music of the Union; Who will care for mother;* and other beautiful songs which the war called forth broke up the sad monotony of many a suffering heart, and beguiled it of the loneliness of its sorrow and bereavement.

IX. THE DISTINCTIVE CHARACTER AND FUTURE MISSION OF OUR NATIONAL SONG.

In the formation of this union, in the re-establishment of this union, our music did effective service, but especially in the last tremendous ordeal was its ministry most helping. It roused the hearts of the people to undertake great things for the salvation of the country ; it called the soldiers to the camping ground ; it inspired them on the weary march ; it nerved them for the battle shock ; it consoled them in their sufferings ; it rose clear and sweet .above the serried hosts of our invincible army on the last great day of victory; it welcomed the noble warriors home ; it now rings, as the flag flies, from the Atlantic to the Pacific shore, from Maine to Mexico. Is its mighty mission over ?

Be pleased to look at it. The leading characteristic of our country's song is determined energy and exulting hope.

The Russian national hymn excites in us the idea of mournful grandeur in accordance with the gigantic power of that vast hyperborean region ; the *Marseillaise, La Parisienne, Mourir pour la patrie,*[1] and Queen Hortensia's *Partant pour la Syrie* of France, awaken tender and affectionate memories of the past; England's national anthem, simple,[2] unaffected, passionless,

[1] Music by F. Alphonse Varney.

[2] *God save the King* appeared originally in the *Gentle-*

seems to be in perfect keeping with the calm
and placid dignity of that people; the Scottish
patriotic airs, as the *Land of the leal, Scots wha
hae wi Wallace bled*, etc., wanting the 7th or
leading note and abounding in minor chords
and cadences, breathe forth the spirit of an
Alpine region full of gloomy caverns which has
lost its king; but the national songs of America,
ringing from the buoyant and elastic spirit of a
people in pursuit of a great destiny, speak out in
every note, in every line, and enkindle in every

---

man's Magazine, Oct., 1745, on the occasion of the landing
of the pretender. Dr. Thomas A. Arne, author of *Arta-
xerxes*, arranged it in parts. The air has been ascribed to
Handel; to Henry Carey who composed the celebrated song
of *Sally in our Alley*, and to others. Dr. Burney maintains
that it was composed for the chapel of James II. The mar-
quise de Créquy in her memoirs published in 1844, says the
music was composed by the celebrated duke of Sully (1560–
1641), and was sung when Louis XIV entered the chapel
of St. Cyr, to the following words written by Madame de
Brinon :

> "Grand Dieu, sauvez le Roi !
> Grand Dieu, venez le Roi !
> Vive le Roi !
> Qui toujours glorieux
> Louis victorieux
> Voyez vos enemis
> Toujours soumis."

The air is sung in Germany and there called *Bundes Lied*.

heart the blessed sentiment of hope.   Hardly
a single minor strain is found in them.   Even

> " Tramp, tramp, tramp, the boys are marching,
>   Cheer up comrades they will come,"[1]

the song of the imprisoned soldier is beaming
in every line with the celestial radiance of hope.
Our songs look away to the brilliant future,
glowing all over as the rainbow with the prophetic inspiration of hope; hope in human
progress, hope in the sweet ministrations of
humanity; hope in the light of woman's love
and beauty; hope in the power of free institu-
tions to sustain themselves; hope in the ulti-
mate triumph of the right; hope in the rising
grandeur of American liberty; hope in the God
of liberty.

Now by the valor of our men ; by the wisdom
of our chieftain ; by the ministration of woman ;
by the enlivening power of music; by the inex-
pressible goodness of God, we are saved as a
nation ; four millions of bondmen have been set
free ; labor has been vindicated ; and the name
of Yankee rendered everlastingly honorable.

---

[1] Words and music by George F. Root.

The walls opposing our success have been demolished; a land of promise, where mines of gold lie packed in between the ribs of the mountains; where rivers of oil flow out of the valleys; a land locked together by the most wonderful net-work of railways and telegraphs; a land broad, fertile, rich, varied, beautiful above all other lands is our inheritance. The golden gates are thrown wide open, and voices call us onward to possess it.

Has national music any part to play? Yes, the grand old songs must still roll on; new songs must be composed; but they must be glowing bright with hope, to stir the blood of the faint-hearted; to cheer up those that fall and falter by the way; to draw the eye to the dear old flag; to repeat the story of the men of 1776; to rehearse the glory of the braves who placed the flag upon the domes of Richmond; to proclaim the illustrious day of freedom; to make the tyrant tremble; to consolidate us into one vast free people; harmonious, high-minded, friendly, hopeful, grateful and aspiring. New times demand new music; let it come in form above the negro melodies from the inspira-

tion of our own warm hearts. Our grand
national hymns we write; our national airs we
borrow; and we take the best; but the genius
of our country now begins to shine brightly forth
in music, even as in her sister arts; let us then
have fresh strains for fresh developments, for
liberty is maintained but by unslumbering vigi-
lance. Strike then from the lyre of freedom
louder, loftier strains, but let the old peal on, for
there is an avenging note in that rollicksome
tune of *Yankee Doodle;* there is solid shot and
shell, as well as hope, in *Hail Columbia;* there
is the invincible pluck of Young America in
the *Star Spangled Banner*, and soldiers marching to these hymns of liberty, lay wide and
clear the track in front of them, unclasping
every bond as they move proudly on to fling
the starry flag of freedom, flaming over the
beloved land.

When the Union flag had come to float once
more above the domes of Richmond, and but a
few nights previous to the assassination of the
illustrious patriot, Abraham Lincoln, he was
called on by the surging crowd around the
White House for a speech.

Rising in the balcony and bowing to the sea of heads in front, he spoke to this effect :

"Gentlemen, I cannot make a speech to-night. I rather feel like hearing music. I want to hear my favorite old tune, *Dixie.* I always did love *Dixie;* and the attorney-general says that we may have it; for *Dixie*, gentlemen, is now our own by right of conquest."

The bands then struck up rapturously the stirring notes of *Dixie, Yankee Doodle, My Maryland*, and the *Star Spangled Banner*, amid the acclamations of the people ; — and so commingling may these strains forever peal in unison, and thus serve to bind this vast birthland of the free into one perfect and harmonious confederation, which under the hero of the nineteenth century and his successors shall ascend to unimagined heights of political, moral, intellectual grandeur, and move this whole world into order by the light of its wisdom, the smile of its beauty, and the song of its love.

FINIS.

10

www.ingramcontent.com/pod-product-compliance
Lightning Source LLC
Chambersburg PA
CBHW020253290326
41930CB00039B/1256